credits

PHOTOGRAPHY
Quail Studio

ART DIRECTION & STYLING
Georgina Brant

DESIGN LAYOUT
Quail Studio

MODEL
Amy Dean

HAIR & MAKEUP
Vanessa - Court-on-Camera Creatives

KNITTERS
Darryl Ingram • Rosie Little • Imogen Reed
Kirsty Bennett • Rebecca Hammond
Cher Marcus • Jackie Freeman • Helen Livermore
Martinette Tindall • Jane O'Reilly

First published in Great Britain in 2021 by
Quail Publishing Limited
Unit 15, Green Farm, Fritwell, Bicester, Oxfordshire,
OX27 7QU
E-mail: info@quailstudio.co.uk

ISBN: 978-1-9162445-7-3

essential
outerwear

ten hand knit designs
in subtle autumnal hues

quail studio

lourdes pattern page 28

demi pattern page 32

esme pattern page 36

soleil pattern page 40

leiana pattern page 44

lana pattern page 48

amore pattern page 52

cici pattern page 56

margo pattern page 60

essential
outerwear

Complete your essential outerwear wardrobe
this season with on-trend knitted pieces,
ideal for throwing over your shoulders before
stepping out into the cold.

From oversized coats and ponchos to neat
waist-length jackets, this collection of cosy
outerwear provides the perfect top layer to
complete your look.

The subtle, autumnal hues of popular Rowan
Yarns combine to create beautiful tonal outfits
imbued with style and sophistication, while
simple shapes and captivating textures will
delight every knitter.

noelle pattern page 64

lourdes

PATTERN PAGE 28

SHOWN IN BIG WOOL | CONCRETE 61

SHOWN IN SOFT BOUCLE | BEAR 604 AND ALPACA SOFT DK | TOFFEE 203

demi

PATTERN PAGE 32

esme

PATTERN PAGE 36

SHOWN IN BRUSHED FLEECE | TARN 254

SHOWN IN KID CLASSIC | CHAMPAGNE 898 AND ALPACA CLASSIC | CHAMPAGNE 127

soleil

PATTERN PAGE 40

leiana

PATTERN PAGE 44

SHOWN IN KID CLASSIC | CLOVER 895

SHOWN IN FELTED TWEED | CAMEL 157 AND KIDSILK HAZE | LUSTRE 686

lana

PATTERN PAGE 48

amore

PATTERN PAGE 52

SHOWN IN BIG WOOL | CACTUS 83

SHOWN IN SOFT BOUCLE | NATURAL 602

cici

PATTERN PAGE 56

margo

PATTERN PAGE 60

SHOWN IN ALPACA SOFT DK | CLASSIC BROWN 204

SHOWN IN FELTED TWEED ARAN | PINE 782

noelle

PATTERN PAGE 64

patterns

lourdes

● ○ ○ ○

SIZE
To fit bust

71-76	81-86	91-97	102-107	112-117	122-127	132-137	142-147	152-157	cm
28-30	32-34	36-38	40-42	44-46	48-50	52-54	56-58	60-62	in

Actual bust measurement of garment

98	108	118	128	138	148	158	168	178	cm
39	43	47	50½	54½	58½	62	66	70	in

YARN
Big Wool

11	11	12	12	13	13	14	14	15	x 100gm

(photographed in Concrete 61)

NEEDLES
1 pair 7mm (no 10/11) (US 10½) needles

TENSION
12 sts and 20 rows to 10cm/4in measured over moss stitch using 7mm (US 10½) needles

EXTRAS
Stitch markers

BACK

Using 7mm (US 10½) needles, cast on 59 [65: 71: 77: 83: 89: 95: 101: 107] sts.
Row 1 (RS): K1, *P1, K1, rep from * to end.
Row 2 (WS): K1, *P1, K1, rep from * to end.
These 2 rows form moss st.
Cont in moss st for a further 10 rows, ending with a RS row.
Next row (RS): Purl.
Next row: Knit.
Beg with row 1, cont in moss st throughout as folls:
Cont straight until back meas 38 [38: 38: 39: 39: 39: 40: 40: 40] cm, ending with RS facing for next row.
Place stitch marker at each end of next RS row to denote start of armholes.
Cont straight until armhole meas 19 [20: 21: 23: 24: 24: 25: 25: 26] cm from markers, ending with RS facing for next row.
Shape shoulder
Cast off 9 [11: 12: 13: 15: 16: 17: 18: 20] sts at beg of next 2 rows, 10 [11: 12: 14: 15: 16: 18: 19: 20] sts at beg of next 2 rows.
Cast off rem 21 [21: 23: 23: 23: 25: 25: 27: 27] sts for back of neck.

LEFT FRONT

Using 7mm (US 10½) needles, cast on 33 [37: 39: 43: 45: 49: 51: 55: 57] sts.
Work in moss st as given for back for 12 rows, ending with RS facing for next row.
Next row (RS): Purl.
Next row: Knit.
Beg with row 1, cont in moss st throughout as folls:
Cont straight until left front meas 38 [38: 38: 39: 39: 39: 40: 40: 40] cm, ending with RS facing for next row.
Place stitch marker at beg of next RS row to denote start of armhole.
Cont straight until armhole meas 1 row less than back to beg of shoulder shaping, ending with WS facing for next row.
Shape neck and shoulder
Next row (WS): Cast off 8 [9: 9: 10: 9: 11: 10: 12: 11] sts, patt to end.
Next row (RS): Cast off 9 [11: 12: 13: 15: 16: 17: 18: 20] sts, patt to end.
Next row (WS): Cast off 3 sts, patt to end.
Next row (RS): Cast off 10 [11: 12: 14: 15: 16: 18: 19: 20] sts, patt to end.
Cast off rem 3 sts.

RIGHT FRONT

Using 7mm (US 10½) needles, cast on 33 [37: 39: 43: 45: 49: 51: 55: 57] sts.
Work in moss st as given for back for 12 rows, ending with RS facing for next row.
Next row (RS): Purl.
Next row: Knit.
Beg with row 1, cont in moss st throughout as folls:
Cont straight until right front meas 38 [38: 38: 39: 39: 39: 40: 40: 40] cm, ending with RS facing for next row.
Place stitch marker at end of next RS row to denote start of armhole.
Cont straight until armhole meas 2 rows less than back to beg of shoulder shaping, ending with RS facing for next row.
Shape neck and shoulder
Next row (RS): Cast off 8 [9: 9: 10: 9: 11: 10: 12: 11] sts, patt to end.
Work 1 row.
Next row (RS): Cast off 3 sts, patt to end.
Next row (WS): Cast off 9 [11: 12: 13: 15: 16: 17: 18: 20] sts, patt to end.
Next row (RS): Cast off 3 sts, patt to end.
Cast off rem 10 [11: 12: 14: 15: 16: 18: 19: 20] sts.

SLEEVES

Using 7mm (US 10½) needles, cast on 25 [27: 27: 27: 29: 29: 29: 31: 31] sts.
Work in moss st as given for back for 16 rows, ending with RS facing for next row.
Next row (RS): Purl.
Next row: Knit.
Beg with row 1, cont in moss st throughout and taking increases into pattern work as folls;
Inc 1 st at each end of 7th and every foll –[-: 4th: 4th: 4th: 4th: 4th: 4th: 4th] row to - [-: 41: 51: 53: 53: 59: 55: 61] sts, then every foll 6th row to 45 [49: 51: 55: 57: 57: 61: 61: 63] sts.
Cont straight until sleeve meas 45 [45: 45: 46: 46: 46: 46: 47: 47] cm, ending with RS facing for next row.
Cast off all sts in patt.

MAKING UP

Block as described on information page.
Join shoulder seams.
Collar
With RS facing and using 7mm (US 10½) needle, beg at right front neck edge, pick and up and knit 17 [18: 18: 19: 19: 19: 19: 21: 21] sts evenly along right front neck edge, 21 [21: 23: 23: 23: 25: 25: 27: 27] sts along back neck and 17 [18: 18: 19: 19: 19: 19: 21: 21] sts along left front edge. 55 [57: 59: 61: 61: 63: 63: 69: 69] sts.
Work in moss st for 10cm/4in, ending with RS facing for next row.
Next row (RS): Purl.
Cast off all sts knitwise.
Side collar edging
With RS facing and using 7mm (US 10½) needle, pick and up and purl 18 sts along one side edge of front collar. Cast off all sts knitwise. Work in same way along other collar edge.
Sew top of sleeve to front and back between armhole markers. Join side and sleeve seams.

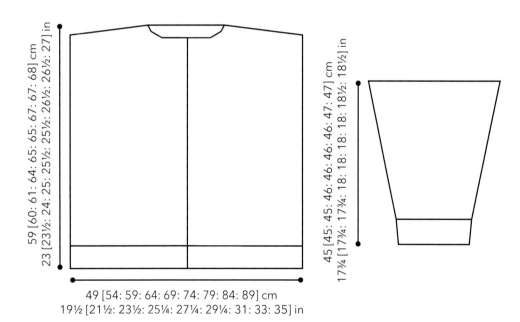

59 [60: 61: 64: 65: 67: 67: 68] cm
23 [23½: 24: 25: 25½: 25½: 26½: 26½: 27] in

45 [45: 45: 46: 46: 46: 47: 47] cm
17¾ [17¾: 17¾: 18: 18: 18: 18½: 18½] in

49 [54: 59: 64: 69: 74: 79: 84: 89] cm
19½ [21½: 23½: 25¼: 27¼: 29¼: 31: 33: 35] in

demi
●●○○

SIZE
To fit bust

71-76	81-86	91-97	102-107	112-117	122-127	132-137	142-147	152-157	cm
28-30	32-34	36-38	40-42	44-46	48-50	52-54	56-58	60-62	in

Actual bust measurement of garment

111	120	131	142	151	162	173	184	195	cm
44	47	51½	56	59½	64	68	72½	77	in

YARN
Soft Boucle
A Bear 604

12	12	13	13	14	14	15	15	16	x 50gm

Alpaca Soft DK
B Toffee 203

3	3	4	4	4	5	5	5	6	x 50gm

NEEDLES
1 pair 5½mm (no 5) (US 9) needles
1 pair 8mm (no 0) (US 11) needles

TENSION
9 sts and 12 rows to 10cm/4in measured over rev st st using triple strand of **Soft Boucle** and 8mm (US 11) needles.
21 sts and 22 rows to 10cm/4in measured over K1, P1 rib using double strand of **Alpaca Soft DK** and 5½mm (US 9) needles.

EXTRAS
Stitch markers
Separating zipper 45 [45: 45: 50: 50: 50: 55: 55: 55] cm long

BACK

Using 5½mm (US 9) needles and double strand of B, cast on 91 [101: 111: 123: 133: 143: 155: 165: 175] sts.

Row 1 (RS): *K1, P1, rep from * end K1.

Row 2 (WS): *P1, K1, rep from * end P1.

These 2 rows form rib.

Cont in rib for 10cm, ending with WS facing for next row.

Dec row (WS): K4 [3: 3: 2: 1: 1: 1: 1: 1], (K2tog) 41 [47: 52: 59: 65: 70: 77: 82: 87] times, K5 [4: 4: 3: 2: 2: 0: 0: 0]. 50 [54: 59: 64: 68: 73: 78: 83: 88] sts. Break both strands of B.

Change to 8mm (US 11) needles and join triple strands of A.

Next row (RS): Purl.

Next row (WS): Knit.

These 2 rows form rev st st.

Cont in rev st st throughout as folls:

Cont straight until back meas 33 [33: 33: 34: 34: 34: 35.5: 35.5: 37] cm from beg, ending with RS facing for next row.

Place stitch marker at each end of next RS row to denote the start of armholes.

Cont straight until armhole meas 19 [20: 22: 23: 25: 26: 27: 28: 30] cm from markers, ending with RS facing for next row.

Cast off all sts.

LEFT FRONT

Using 5½mm (US 9) needles and double strand of B, cast on 45 [49: 57: 61: 67: 71: 77: 81: 87] sts.

Work in rib as given for back for 10cm, ending with WS facing for next row.

Dec row (WS): K2 [2: 1: 1: 1: 1: 1: 1: 1], (K2tog) 20 [22: 27: 29: 33: 35: 38: 39: 43] times, K3 [3: 2: 2: 0: 0: 0: 2: 0]. 25 [27: 30: 32: 34: 36: 39: 42: 44] sts. Break both strands of B.

Change to 8mm (US 11) needles and join triple strands of A.

Cont in rev st st throughout as folls:

Cont straight until left front meas 33 [33: 33: 34: 34: 34: 35.5: 35.5: 37] cm from beg, ending with RS facing for next row.

Place stitch marker at beg of next RS row to denote the start of armhole.

Cont straight until 10 rows less have been worked than on back to beg of shoulder shaping, end with RS facing for next row.

Work 1 row.

Shape neck

Next row (WS): Cast off 4 [4: 5: 5: 5: 5: 6: 7: 7] sts (neck edge), knit to end. 21 [23: 25: 27: 29: 31: 33: 35: 37] sts.

Next row (RS): Purl last 3 sts, p2tog, p1. 20 [22: 24: 26: 28: 30: 32: 34: 36] sts.

Knit 1 row.

Rep last 2 rows 3 times more. Cast off rem 17 [19: 21: 23: 25: 27: 29: 31: 33] sts for shoulder.

RIGHT FRONT

Using 5½mm (US 9) needles and double strand of B, cast on 45 [49: 57: 61: 67: 71: 77: 81: 87] sts.

Work in rib as given for back for 10cm, ending with WS facing for next row.

Dec row (WS): K2 [2: 1: 1: 1: 1: 1: 1: 1], (K2tog) 20 [22: 27: 29: 33: 35: 38: 39: 43] times, K3 [3: 2: 2: 0: 0: 0: 2: 0]. 25 [27: 30: 32: 34: 36: 39: 42: 44] sts. Break both strands of B.

Change to 8mm (US 11) needles and join triple strands of A.

Cont in rev st st throughout as folls:

Cont straight until right front meas 33 [33: 33: 34: 34: 34: 35.5: 35.5: 37] cm from beg, ending with RS facing for next row.

Place stitch marker at end of next RS row to denote the start of armhole.

Cont straight until 10 rows less have been worked than on back to beg of shoulder shaping, end with RS facing for next row.

Shape neck
Next row (RS): Cast off 4 [4: 5: 5: 5: 5: 6: 7: 7] sts (neck edge), purl to end. 21 [23: 25: 27: 29: 31: 33: 35: 37] sts.
Knit 1 row.
Next row (RS): P1, P2tog, purl to end. 20 [22: 24: 26: 28: 30: 32: 34: 36] sts.
Knit 1 row.
Rep last 2 rows 3 times more. Cast off rem 17 [19: 21: 23: 25: 27: 29: 31: 33] sts for shoulder.

SLEEVES
Using 5½mm (US 9) needles and double strand of B, cast on 43 [43: 45: 45: 49: 49: 51: 51: 55] sts.
Work in rib as given for back for 10cm, ending with WS facing for next row.
Dec row (WS): Purl and dec 8 [6: 5: 3: 4: 2: 2: 0: 1] sts evenly across. 35 [37: 40: 42: 45: 47: 49: 51: 54] sts.
Break both strands of B.
Change to 8mm (US 11) needles and join triple strands of A.
Cont in rev st st throughout as folls:
Cont straight until sleeve meas 48 [51: 51: 51: 51: 52: 52: 52: 52] cm from beg, ending with RS facing for next row.
Cast off all sts loosely.

MAKING UP
Block as described on information page.
Join shoulder seams using back stitch, or mattress stitch if preferred.
Collar
With RS facing and using 8mm (US 11) needles and triple strand of A, beg at right front neck edge, pick up and knit 12 [12: 13: 13: 13: 13: 14: 15: 15] sts along right front neck edge, 16 [16: 17: 18: 18: 19: 20: 21: 22] sts along back neck, 12 [12: 13: 13: 13: 13: 14: 15: 15] sts along left front neck edge. 40 [40: 43: 44: 44: 45: 48: 51: 52] sts.
Begin with a knit (WS) row, work in rev st st for 15cm, end with RS facing for next row.
Turning ridge row (RS): Knit.
Beg with a knit (WS) row, work in rev st st for 15cm. Cast off sts loosely.
Fold collar in half at turning ridge row to WS and sew in place around neck edge.
Sew top of sleeve to front and back between markers. Sew side and sleeve seams.

Left Front zipper band
With RS facing and using 5½mm (US 9) needles and double strand of B, beg just below neck shaping, pick up and knit 90 [92: 94: 100: 102: 106: 111: 113: 118] sts evenly along straight edge of left front.
Cast off knitwise on WS.
Right Front zipper band
With RS facing, beg at lower edge, using 5.5mm (US 9) needles and double strand of B, pick up and knit 90 [92: 94: 100: 102: 106: 111: 113: 118] sts evenly along straight edge of right front, ending just below neck shaping. Cast off knitwise on WS.
Sew in zipper to WS of zipper band.

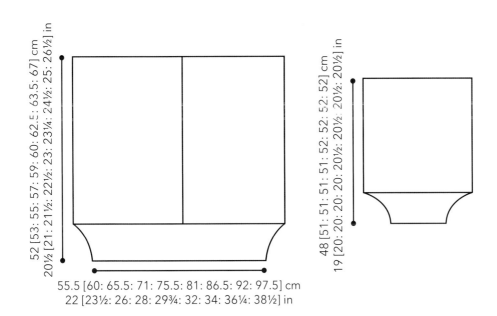

52 [53: 55: 57: 59: 60: 62: 63.5: 67] cm
20½ [21: 21½: 22½: 23: 23¼: 24½: 25: 26½] in

55.5 [60: 65.5: 71: 75.5: 81: 86.5: 92: 97.5] cm
22 [23½: 26: 28: 29¾: 32: 34: 36¼: 38½] in

48 [51: 51: 51: 52: 52: 52: 52: 52] cm
19 [20: 20: 20: 20: 20½: 20½: 20½: 20½] in

esme
● ○ ○ ○

SIZE
To fit bust

71-76	81-86	91-97	102-107	112-117	122-127	132-137	142-147	152-157	cm
28-30	32-34	36-38	40-42	44-46	48-50	52-54	56-58	60-62	in

Actual bust measurement of garment

105	117	126	135	145	154	166	175	185	cm
41½	46	50	53	57	60½	65½	69	73	in

YARN
Brushed Fleece

10	10	10	11	11	12	12	13	13	x 50gm

(photographed in Tarn 254)

NEEDLES
1 x 6mm (no 4) (US 10) circular needle, 80cm/32in long

TENSION
13 sts and 19 rows to 10cm/4in measured over st st using 6mm (US 10) needles.
14 sts and 19 rows to 10cm/4in measured over K1, P1 rib using 6mm (US 10) needles.

BACK

Using 6mm (US 10) circular needle, cast on 73 [81: 87: 95: 101: 109: 115: 123: 129] sts. Do *not* join; work back and forth in rows.
Row 1 (RS): K1, *P1, K1, rep from * to end.
Row 2: P1, *K1, P1, rep from * to end.
These *2* rows form rib.
Cont in rib for 8cm, ending with WS facing for next row.
Next row (WS): Purl and dec 5 [5: 5: 7: 7: 9: 7: 9: 9] sts evenly spaced across. 68 [76: 82: 88: 94: 100: 108: 114: 120] sts.
Beg with a K row, cont in st st throughout as folls:
Cont straight until back meas 33cm, ending with RS facing for next row.

Shape sleeves

Cast on 1 st at beg of next 12 [12: 12: 12: 12: 12: 14: 14: 14] rows, 2 sts at beg of the foll 14 [14: 14: 14: 16: 16: 16: 16: 16] rows, and 9 sts at beg of the foll 2 rows. 126 [134: 140: 146: 156: 162: 172: 178: 184] sts.
Cont straight until sleeve meas 28 [30: 32: 33: 34: 35: 36: 36: 36] cm from last sleeve cast-on, ending with RS facing for next row.
Cast off all sts, marking centre 24 [26: 26: 26: 28: 28: 30: 30: 32] sts for back neck opening.

LEFT FRONT

Using 6mm (US 10) circular needle, cast on 43 [47: 49: 53: 57: 59: 63: 67: 71] sts. Do *not* join; work back and forth in rows.
Work in rib as given for back for 8cm, ending with WS facing for next row.
Next row (WS): Purl and dec 3 [3: 3: 4: 4: 4: 4: 4: 6] sts evenly spaced across. 40 [44: 46: 49: 53: 55: 59: 63: 65] sts.
Beg with a K row, cont in st st throughout as folls:
Cont straight until left front meas 33cm, ending with RS facing for next row.

Shape sleeve and neck

Next row (RS): Cast on 1 st (sleeve edge), knit to last 3 sts, K2tog, K1 (neck dec). Cont to work sleeves incs at sleeve edge as for back, and dec 1 st at neck edge on every foll 4th row 15 [15: 11: 10: 15: 10: 12: 14: 13] times, then every foll 6th row 2 [3: 6: 7: 4: 8: 7: 6: 7] times. 51 [54: 57: 60: 64: 67: 71: 74: 76] sts.
Cont straight until sleeve meas 28 [30: 32: 33: 34: 35: 36: 36: 36] cm from last sleeve cast-on, ending with RS facing for next row.
Cast off all sts.

RIGHT FRONT

Using 6mm (US 10) circular needle, cast on 43 [47: 49: 53: 57: 59: 63: 67: 71] sts. Do *not* join; work back and forth in rows.
Work in rib as given for back for 8cm, ending with WS facing for next row.
Next row (WS): Purl and dec 3 [3: 3: 4: 4: 4: 4: 4: 6] sts evenly spaced across. 40 [44: 46: 49: 53: 55: 59: 63: 65] sts.
Beg with a K row, cont in st st throughout as folls:
Cont straight until right front meas 33cm, ending with RS facing for next row.

Shape neck and sleeve

Next row (RS): K1, SKP (neck dec), knit to end.
Next row (WS): Cast on 1 st (sleeve edge), purl to end.
Cont to work neck decs and sleeve incs as for left front reversing shapings. 51 [54: 57: 60: 64: 67: 71: 74: 76] sts.
Cont straight until sleeve meas 28 [30: 32: 33: 34: 35: 36: 36: 36] cm from last sleeve cast-on, ending with RS facing for next row.
Cast off all sts.

MAKING UP

Block as described on information page.

Join shoulder seams.

Sleeve band

With RS facing and 6mm (US 10) circular needle, pick up and knit 77 [81: 87: 91: 93: 97: 99: 99: 99] sts evenly along sleeve edge of front and back. Do *not* join; work back and forth in rows.

Work in rib as given for back for 8cm.

Cast off loosely in rib.

Work band along second sleeve in same way.

Collar

With RS facing and 6mm (US 10) circular needle, beg at right front neck shaping, pick and up and knit 61 [64: 66: 68: 69: 71: 74: 75: 77] sts evenly along right front neck edge, 25 [27: 27: 27: 29: 29: 31: 31: 33] sts along back neck and 61 [64: 66: 68: 69: 71: 74: 75: 77] sts along left front neck edge to start of neck shaping. 147 [155: 159: 163: 167: 171: 179: 181: 187] sts. Do *not* join; work back and forth in rows.

Work in rib as given for back for 24cm.

Cast off loosely in rib.

Join side and sleeve seams.

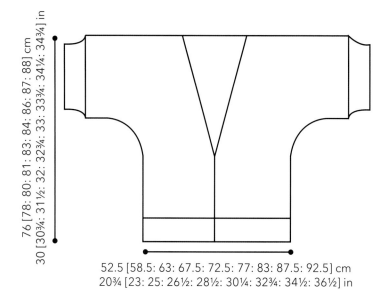

76 [78: 80: 81: 83: 84: 86: 87: 88] cm
30 [30¾: 31½: 32: 32¾: 33: 33¾: 34¼: 34¾] in

52.5 [58.5: 63: 67.5: 72.5: 77: 83: 87.5: 92.5] cm
20¾ [23: 25: 26½: 28½: 30¼: 32¾: 34½: 36½] in

soleil
● ○ ○ ○

SIZE

To fit bust

71-76	81-86	91-97	102-107	112-117	122-127	132-137	142-147	152-157	cm
28-30	32-34	36-38	40-42	44-46	48-50	52-54	56-58	60-62	in

Actual bust measurement of garment

108	117	128	137	148	157	169	179	187	cm
43	46	50½	54	58½	62	66	70	74	in

YARN

Kid Classic
A Champagne 898

7	7	8	8	9	9	10	10	11	x 50gm

Alpaca Classic
B Champagne 127

7	7	8	8	9	9	10	10	11	x 25gm

NEEDLES

1 pair 5½mm (no 5) (US 9) needles
1 x 5½mm (no 5) (US 9) circular needle, 80cm/32in long

TENSION

14 sts and 16 rows to 10cm/4in measured over rev st st using 5½mm (US 9) needles, holding 1 strand of each together.

EXTRAS

Stitch holders
Stitch markers

BACK

Using 5½mm (US 9) needles and 1 strand of A and B held together, cast on 76 [82: 90: 96: 104: 110: 118: 125: 131] sts.

Knit 4 rows.

Next row (RS): Purl.

Next row (WS): Knit.

These 2 rows form rev st st.

Cont in rev st st throughtout as folls:

Cont straight until back meas 45cm, ending with RS facing for next row.

Place stitch marker each end of next RS row to denote the start of armholes.

Cont straight until armhole meas 22 [23: 24: 24: 25.5: 27: 27: 28: 29.5] cm from markers, ending with RS facing for next row.

Shape shoulders

Cast off 3 [3: 3: 4: 4: 5: 5: 5: 6] sts at beg of next 14 [10: 2: 12: 6: 16: 10: 4: 16] rows and 4 [4: 4: 5: 5: 0: 6: 6: 0] sts at beg of next 2 [6: 14: 4: 10: 0: 6: 12: 0] rows.

Cast off rem 26 [28: 28: 28: 30: 30: 32: 33: 35] sts for back neck.

LEFT FRONT

Using 5½mm (US 9) needles and 1 strand of A and B held together, cast on 25 [27: 31: 34: 37: 40: 43: 46: 48] sts.

Knit 4 rows.

Beg with a P row, cont in rev st st throughtout as folls:

Cont straight until left front meas 45cm, ending with RS facing for next row.

Place marker at beg of next RS row to denote the start of armhole.

Cont straight until armhole meas 22 [23: 24: 24: 25.5: 27: 27: 28: 29.5] cm from marker, ending with RS facing for next row.

Shape shoulder

Cast off 3 [3: 3: 4: 4: 5: 5: 5: 6] sts 7 [5: 1: 6: 3: 8: 5: 2: 8] times and 4 [4: 4: 5: 5: 0: 6: 6: 0] sts 1 [3: 7: 2: 5: 0: 3: 6: 0] times.

RIGHT FRONT

Using 5½mm (US 9) needles and 1 strand of A and B held together, cast on 25 [27: 31: 34: 37: 40: 43: 46: 48] sts.

Knit 4 rows.

Beg with a P row, cont in rev st st throughtout as folls:

Cont straight until right front meas 45cm, ending with RS facing for next row.

Place marker at end of next RS row to denote the start of armhole.

Cont straight until armhole meas 22 [23: 24: 24: 25.5: 27: 27: 28: 29.5] cm from marker, ending with WS facing for next row.

Shape shoulder

Cast off 3 [3: 3: 4: 4: 5: 5: 5: 6] sts 7 [5: 1: 6: 3: 8: 5: 2: 8] times and 4 [4: 4: 5: 5: 0: 6: 6: 0] sts 1 [3: 7: 2: 5: 0: 3: 6: 0] times.

SLEEVES

Using 5½mm (US 9) needles and 1 strand of A and B held together, cast on 32 [32: 34: 34: 36: 36: 38: 39: 39] sts.

Knit 4 rows.

Beg with a P row, cont in rev st st throughtout as folls:

Inc 1 st each end of 2nd and every foll alt row to 42 [42: 48: 48: 52: 60: 58: 61: 69] sts, then every foll 4th row to 62 [64: 68: 68: 72: 76: 76: 79: 83] sts.

Cont straight until sleeve meas 38 [40: 40: 40: 42: 42: 42: 43: 43] cm, ending with RS facing for next row.

Cast off all sts loosely.

MAKING UP

Block as described on information page.

Join shoulder seams using back stitch, or mattress stitch if preferred.

Right Front and neck band

With RS facing and using 5½mm (US 9) circular needle and 1 strand of A and B held together, beg at lower right front edge, pick up and knit 120 [119: 125: 125: 130: 130: 129: 134: 134] sts along right front edge, 13 [13: 14: 14: 15: 15: 16: 17: 17] sts along one half of back neck to centre back. 133 [133: 139: 139: 145: 145: 145: 151: 151] sts.

Row 1 (WS): P2, *K3, P3, rep from * to last 5 sts, K3, P2.

Row 2: K2, *P3, K3, rep from * to last 5 sts, P3, K2.

These 2 rows form rib.

Rep last 2 rows until band meas 19 [20: 20: 20: 22: 22: 23: 24: 25] cm, ending with RS facing for next row.

Cast off sts loosely in rib.

Left Front and neck band

With RS facing and using 5½mm (US 9) circular needle and 1 strand of A and B held together, beg at centre back neck, pick up and knit 13 [13: 14: 14: 15: 15: 16: 17: 17] sts along rem half of back neck, 120 [119: 125: 125: 130: 130: 129: 134: 134] sts along left front edge. 133 [133: 139: 139: 145: 145: 145: 151: 151] sts.

Complete as right front band.

Sew ends of neckband tog at centre back neck.

Using markers as a guide, sew in sleeves.

Sew side and sleeve seams.

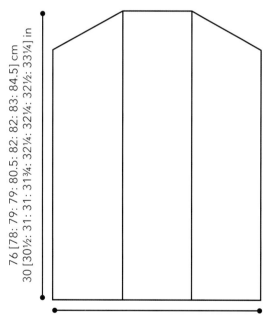

54 [58.5: 64: 68.5: 74: 78.5: 84.5: 89.5: 93.5] cm
21½ [23: 25½: 27: 29¼: 31: 33¼: 35¼: 36¾] in

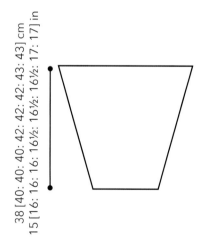

leiana

●●○○

SIZE

To fit bust

71-76	81-86	91-97	102-107	112-117	122-127	132-137	142-147	152-157	cm
28-30	32-34	36-38	40-42	44-46	48-50	52-54	56-58	60-62	in

Actual bust measurement of garment

90	99	111	120	133	141	154	162	175	cm
36	39	45	47½	52	55½	60½	64	69	in

YARN

Kid Classic

10	11	11	12	12	13	13	14	14	x 50gm

(photographed in Clover 895)

NEEDLES

2 x 5mm (no 6) (US 8) circular needles, 80cm/32in long

TENSION

19 sts and 25 rows to 10cm/4in measured over K2, P2 rib (blocked) using 5mm (US 8) needles.
20 sts and 38 rows to 10cm/4in measured over garter stitch using 5mm (US 8) needles.
19 sts and 25 rows to 10cm/4in measured over st st using 5mm (US 8) needles.

EXTRAS

Stitch holders
Stitch markers

NOTE

When working the shawl collar, two circular needles are used. Wrap and turn is *not used* when working short rows in garter stitch.

BACK

Using 5mm (US 8) circular needle, cast on 86 [94: 106: 114: 126: 134: 146: 154: 166] sts. Do *not* join; work back and forth in rows.

Row 1 (RS): K2, *P2, K2, rep from * to end.

Row 2: P2, *K2, P2, rep from * to end.

These 2 rows form rib pattern.

Cont in rib patt for 5cm, ending with RS facing for next row.

Next row (RS): Knit.

Cont in garter st (knit every row) until back meas 16cm, ending with RS facing for next row.

Beg with a K row, cont in st st throughout as folls:

Cont straight until back meas 28 [28: 28: 28: 29: 29: 29: 30: 30] cm, ending with RS facing for next row.

Shape sleeves

Cast on 2 sts at beg of next 32 [32: 34: 34: 34: 38: 38: 38: 40] rows, 4 [5: 4: 4: 4: 3: 3: 3: 3] sts at beg of the foll 4 [4: 4: 4: 4: 4: 4: 4] rows, and 30 sts at beg of the foll 2 rows. 226 [238: 250: 258: 270: 282: 294: 302: 318] sts.

Next row (RS): Knit.

Next row (WS): K30, purl to last 30 sts, K30.

These 2 rows form pattern.

Cont in patt until sleeve meas 19 [20: 20: 21: 21: 21: 23: 23: 24] cm from last sleeve cast-on, ending with RS facing for next row.

Shape shoulders and back neck

Cast off 11 [12: 13: 13: 14: 15: 15: 16: 17] sts at beg of next 8 [14: 14: 10: 14: 10: 10: 12: 12] rows, 12 [13: 12: 14: 13: 14: 16: 15: 16] sts at beg of the foll 8 [2: 2: 6: 2: 6: 6: 4: 4] rows.

Cast off rem 42 [44: 44: 44: 48: 48: 48: 50: 50] sts for back neck.

FRONT

Work as for back until sleeve increases are complete, ending with RS facing for next row. 226 [238: 250: 258: 270: 282: 294: 302: 318] sts.

Next row (RS): Knit.

Next row (WS): K30, purl to last 30 sts, k30.

These 2 rows form pattern.

Mark centre 24 [26: 26: 26: 30: 30: 30: 32: 32] sts.

Shape neck

Next row (RS): Patt to centre 24 [26: 26: 26: 30: 30: 30: 32: 32] sts and turn, leaving rem sts on a holder. Work each side of neck separately.

Work 1 row.

Next row (RS): Patt to last 3 sts, K2tog, K1. 100 [105: 111: 115: 119: 125: 131: 134: 142] sts.

Work 5 rows.

Rep last 6 rows until 92 [97: 103: 107: 111: 117: 123: 126: 134] sts remain.

Cont straight, if necessary, until sleeve meas 19 [20: 20: 21: 21: 21: 23: 23: 24] cm from last sleeve cast-on, ending with RS facing for next row.

Shape shoulders and back neck

Cast off from shoulder edge (beg of RS rows) 11 [12: 13: 13: 14: 15: 15: 16: 17] sts 4 [7: 7: 5: 7: 5: 5: 6: 6] times, 12 [13: 12: 14: 13: 14: 16: 15: 16] sts 4 [1: 1: 3: 1: 3: 3: 2: 2] times.

Return to sts left on holder, rejoin yarn with RS facing and cast off centre 24 [26: 26: 26: 30: 30: 30: 32: 32] sts, patt to end. 101 [106: 112: 116: 120: 126: 132: 135: 143] sts.

Complete to match first side, reversing shapings.

MAKING UP

Block as described on information page.

Join shoulder seams using mattress stitch.

Sleeve band

With RS facing and using 5mm (US 8) circular needle, pick up and knit 74 [78: 78: 82: 82: 82: 86: 86: 90] sts evenly along sleeve edge of front and back. Do *not* join; work back and forth in rows.

Beg with row 2, work in rib as given for back for 5cm, ending with RS facing for next row.

Cast off **loosely** in rib.

Work other side to match.

Collar

With RS facing and using 5mm (US 8) circular needle, beg at inside right front neck edge, pick and up and knit 55 [58: 58: 60: 60: 60: 62: 62: 66] sts evenly along right front neck edge, 42 [44: 44: 44: 48: 48: 48: 50: 50] sts along back neck and 55 [58: 58: 60: 60: 60: 62: 62: 66] sts along left front edge. 152 [160: 160: 164: 168: 168: 172: 174: 182] sts.

Working back and forth using 2nd circular needle, work in garter st for 12.5 [13.5: 13.5: 13.5: 16: 16: 16: 17: 17] cm, ending with RS facing for next row.

Beg short row shaping

Short row 1 (RS): Knit until 8 sts rem on LH needle, turn work.
Short row 2 (WS): Knit until 8 sts rem on LH needle, turn work.
Short row 3: Knit until 16 sts rem on LH needle, turn work.
Short row 4: Knit until 16 sts rem on LH needle, turn work.
Short row 5: Knit until 20 sts rem on LH needle, turn work.
Short row 6: Knit until 20 sts rem on LH needle, turn work.

Cont to work short rows as established, leaving 4 sts more unworked at end of each row for the foll 16 rows.

Next 2 rows: Work to end of each row.

Cast off sts.

Sew side of left front collar to centre cast-off front neck sts. Overlap side of right front collar and sew in place along centre front.

Join side and sleeve seams.

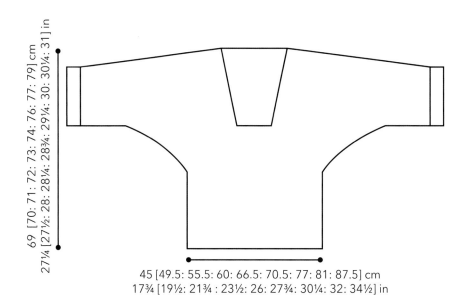

69 [70: 71: 72: 73: 74: 76: 77: 79] cm
27¼ [27½: 28: 28¼: 28¾: 29¼: 30: 30¼: 31] in

45 [49.5: 55.5: 60: 66.5: 70.5: 77: 81: 87.5] cm
17¾ [19½: 21¾ : 23½: 26: 27¾: 30¼: 32: 34½] in

lana

● ○ ○ ○

SIZE

To fit bust

| 71-97 | 102-127 | 132-147 | cm |
| 28-38 | 40-50 | 52-62 | in |

Actual width at lower edge of back (or front)

| 82 | 95 | 110 | cm |
| 32½ | 37½ | 43½ | in |

YARN

Felted Tweed
A Camel 157

| 7 | 8 | 9 | x 50gm |

Kidsilk Haze
B Lustre 686

| 6 | 7 | 8 | x 25gm |

NEEDLES

1 pair 4½mm (no 7) (US 7) needles
1 pair 5mm (no 6) (US 8) needles
1 x 5mm (no 6) (US 7) circular needle, 40cm/16in long

TENSION

19 sts and 30 rows to 10cm/4in measured over st st using 5mm (US 8) needles and one strand each of A and B held together.

EXTRAS

Stitch marker

SPECIAL ABBREVIATIONS
Make One (M1)
Insert tip of LH needle from front to back under the strand between the last stitch worked and the next stitch on the needle. Knit into the back loop of this strand – 1 stitch increased.

NOTES
This poncho is made is four pieces: two fronts and two backs, then sewn together to form the poncho. The rev st st lower hem is then picked up and worked down.

RIGHT BACK PANEL
Using 5mm (US 8) needles and 1 strand of A and B held together, cast on 78 [90: 104] sts.
Beg with a K row, cont in st st throughout as folls:
Cont straight until right back panel meas 24 [22: 20] cm, ending with RS facing for next row.
Shape arm opening
Dec row (RS) K1, SKP, knit to end. 77 [89: 103] sts.
Next row: Purl.
Rep last 2 rows 4 times more. 73 [85: 99] sts.
Work straight until arm opening meas 13 [15: 17] cm, ending with RS facing for next row.
Inc row (RS) K1, M1, knit to end. 74 [86: 100] sts.
Next row: Purl.
Rep last 2 rows 4 times more. 78 [90: 104] sts.
Shape shoulder and neck
Next row (RS): Cast off 2 sts, knit to end. 76 [88: 102] sts.
Next row: Purl.
Rep last 2 rows 15 [22: 31] times more. 46 [44: 40] sts.
Next row (RS) Cast off 1 st, knit to end. 45 [43: 39] sts.
Next row: Purl.
Rep last 2 rows 25 [21: 15] times more. 20 [22: 24] sts.
Next row (RS) Cast off 1 st, knit to end.
Next row (WS) Cast off 5 [7: 7] sts, purl to end. 14 [14: 16] sts.
Next row Cast off 1 st, knit to end.
Next row Cast off 6 [6: 7] sts, purl to end. 7 [7: 8] sts.
Rep last 2 rows once more.

LEFT BACK PANEL
Using 5mm (US 8) needles and 1 strand of A and B held together, cast on 78 [90: 104] sts.
Beg with a K row, cont in st st throughout as folls:
Cont straight until left back panel meas 24 [22: 20] cm, ending with RS facing for next row.
Shape arm opening
Dec row (RS): K to last 3 sts, K2tog, K1. 77 [89: 103] sts.
Next row: Purl.
Rep last 2 rows 4 times more. 73 [85: 99] sts.
Work straight until arm opening meas 13 [15: 17] cm, ending with RS facing for next row.
Inc row (RS): K to last st, M1, K1. 74 [86: 100] sts.
Next row: Purl.
Rep last 2 rows 4 times more. 78 [90: 104] sts.
Next row (RS): Knit.
Shape shoulder and neck
Next row (WS): Cast off 2 sts, purl to end. 76 [88: 102] sts.
Next row: Knit.
Rep last 2 rows 15 [22: 31] times more. 46 [44: 40] sts.
Next row (WS): Cast off 1 st, purl to end. 45 [43: 39] sts.
Next row: Knit.
Rep last 2 rows 25 [21: 15] times more. 20 [22: 24] sts.
Next row (WS): Cast off 1 st, purl to end.
Next row (RS): Cast off 5 [7: 7] sts, knit to end. 14 [14: 16] sts.
Next row: Cast off 1 st, purl to end.
Next row: Cast off 6 [6: 7] sts, knit to end. 7 [7: 8] sts.
Rep last 2 rows once more.

LEFT FRONT PANEL
Work same as right back panel until end of arm opening, ending with RS facing for next row. 78 [90: 104] sts.
Shape shoulder and neck
Next row (RS): Cast off 2 sts, knit to end. 76 [88: 102] sts.
Next row: Purl.
Rep last 2 rows 15 [22: 31] times more. 46 [44: 40] sts.
Next row (RS): Cast off 1 st, knit to end. 45 [43: 39] sts.
Next row: Purl.
Rep last 2 rows 19 [15: 9] times more. 26 [28: 30] sts.
Next row (RS): Cast off 1 st, knit to end.
Next row (WS): Cast off 9 [11: 13] sts, purl to end. 16 sts.
Next row: Cast off 1 st, knit to end.
Next row: Cast off 1 st, purl to end. 14 sts.
Rep last 2 rows 7 times more.

RIGHT FRONT PANEL
Work same as left back panel until end of arm opening, ending with RS facing for next row. 78 [90: 104] sts.
Next row (RS): Knit.
Shape shoulder and neck
Next row (WS): Cast off 2 sts, purl to end. 76 [88: 102] sts.
Next row: Knit.
Rep last 2 rows 15 [22: 31] times more. 46 [44: 40] sts.
Next row (WS): Cast off 1 st, purl to end. 45 [43: 39] sts.
Next row: Knit.
Rep last 2 rows 19 [15: 9] times more. 26 [28: 30] sts.
Next row (WS): Cast off 1 st, purl to end.
Next row (RS): Cast off 9 [11: 13] sts, knit to end. 16 sts.
Next row: Cast off 1 st, purl to end.
Next row: Cast off 1 st, knit to end. 14 sts.
Rep last 2 rows 7 times more.

MAKING UP
Block as described on information page.
Join front and back pieces together at the centre front.
Join shoulder seams using back stitch, or mattress stitch if preferred.
Arm opening border
With RS facing and using 4½mm (US 7) needles and 1 strand of A and B held together, pick up and knit 70 [78: 90] sts evenly along front and back arm opening on one side.
Next row (RS): * K1, P1, rep from * to end.
Last row forms rib.
Cont in rib until border meas 2.5cm, ending with RS facing for next row.
Cast off loosely in rib.
Work other side to match.
Lower edge hem
With RS facing and using 5mm (US 8) needles and 1 strand of A and B held together, pick up and knit 156 [180: 206] sts along lower edge of back.
Beg with a K row (WS), work in rev st st for 7cm, ending with RS facing for next row.
Cast off loosely purlwise.
Work in same way along lower edge of front.
Collar
With RS facing and using 5mm (US 8) circular needle and 1 strand of A and B held together, pick up and knit 38 [42: 46] sts along back neck and 46 [50: 54] sts along front neck. 84 [92: 100] sts.
Join and place marker for beg of rnd.

Rnd 1: Knit

Last rnd forms st st.

Cont in st st rnds for 16cm.

Cast off loosely knitwise.

Join side seams.

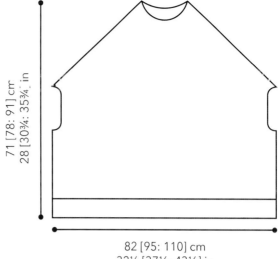

71 [78: 91] cm
28 [30¾: 35¾] in

82 [95: 110] cm
32¼ [37½: 43¼] in

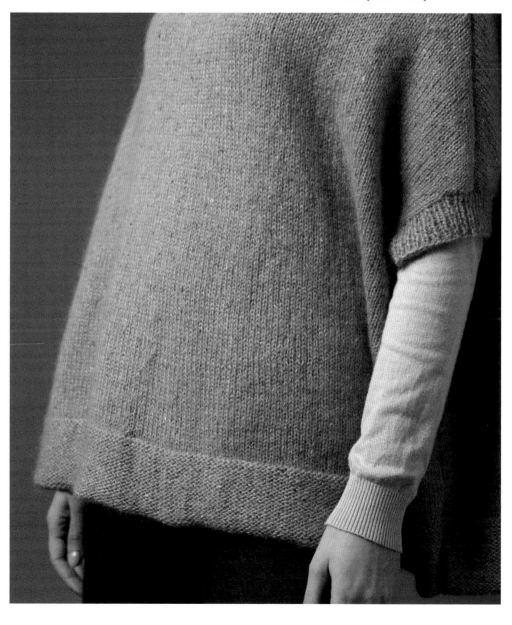

amore
● ● ○ ○

SIZE

To fit bust

71-76	81-86	91-97	102-107	112-117	122-127	132-137	142-147	152-157	cm
28-30	32-34	36-38	40-42	44-46	48-50	52-54	56-58	60-62	in

Actual bust measurement of garment

102	112	122	132	142	152	162	172	182	cm
40	44	48	52	56	60	64	67¾	71¾	in

YARN

Big Wool

13	13	14	14	15	15	16	16	17	x 100gm

(photographed in Cactus 83)

NEEDLES

1 x 7mm (no 2) (US 10½) circular needle, 80cm/32in long
2 x 9mm (no 00) (US 13) circular needles, 80cm/32in long

TENSION

12 sts and 16 rows to 10cm measured over K1, P1 rib using 7mm (US 10½) needle.
8 sts and 20 rows to 10cm measured over brioche rib using 9mm (US 13) needle.

EXTRAS

Stitch holders
Stitch markers

SPECIAL ABBREVIATIONS

Knit 1 below (K1b)
Insert your right needle through the stitch below the first st on the left needle, bring the yarn through and lift st off left needle.

Make Two (M2KP)
With the needle tip, lift the strand between the last stitch worked and the next stitch on left-hand needle, knit into back of strand, then purl into front of same strand. One knit and one purl stitch have been increased.

Make Two (M2PK)
With the needle tip, lift the strand between the last stitch worked and the next stitch on left-hand needle, purl into front of strand, then knit into back of same strand. One purl and one knit stitch have been increased.

S2KP
Slip 2 sts knitwise as if to K2tog, K1, pass slipped sts over K1. 2 sts dec'd.

BACK
Using 7mm (US 10½) circular needle, cast on 61 [67: 73: 79: 85: 91: 97: 103: 109] sts. Do *not* join; work back and forth in rows.
Row 1 (RS): K1, *P1, K1, rep from * to end.
Row 2 (WS): P1, *K1, P1, rep from * to end.
These 2 rows form K1, P1 rib.
Cont in rib for 6cm, end with WS facing for the next row.
Dec row (WS): P1, (S2KP, P1, K1b, P1) 10 [11: 12: 13: 14: 15: 16: 17: 18] times. 41 [45: 49: 53: 57: 61: 65: 69: 73] sts.
Change to 9mm (US 13) circular needle.
Now work in brioche rib patt as folls:
Row 1 (RS): K1, *P1, K1, rep from * to end.
Row 2 (WS): P1, *K1b, P1, rep from * to end.
Row 3: K1, *P1, K1b, rep from * to last st, K1.
Rows 2 and 3 form brioche rib patt.
Cont straight until back meas 38 [38: 38: 38: 39.5: 39.5: 41: 41: 41] cm, ending with RS facing for next row.
Place stitch marker at each end of next RS row to denote start of armholes.
Cont straight until armhole meas 23 [24: 25.5: 25.5: 26.5 28: 28: 29: 30.5] cm from markers, ending with RS facing for next row.
Shape shoulders
Cast off 10 [12: 14: 16: 18: 20: 22: 24: 26] sts at beg of next 2 rows. Place rem 21 sts on holder for back neck.

LEFT FRONT
Using 7mm (US 10½) circular needle, cast on 31 [33: 37: 39: 43: 45: 49: 51: 55] sts. Do *not* join; work back and forth in rows.
Work in K1, P1 rib as given for back for 6cm, ending with WS facing for the next row.
Dec row (WS): P1, (K1b, P1) 0 [1: 0: 1: 0: 1: 0: 1: 0] time, (S2KP, P1 K1b, P1) 5 [5: 6: 6: 7: 7: 8: 8: 9] times. 21 [23: 25: 27: 29: 31: 33: 35: 37] sts.
Change to 9mm (US 13) circular needle.
Beg with row 1, work in brioche rib patt as folls:
Cont straight until left front meas 38 [38: 38: 38: 39.5: 39.5: 41: 41: 41] cm, ending with RS facing for next row.
Place stitch marker at beg of next RS row to denote start of armhole.
Cont straight until armhole meas 23 [24: 25.5: 25.5: 26.5 28: 28: 29: 30.5] cm from marker, ending RS facing for next row.
Shape shoulders
Cast off 10 [12: 14: 16: 18: 20: 22: 24: 26] sts at beg of next RS row. Place rem 11 sts on holder for neck.

RIGHT FRONT

Using 7mm (US 10½) circular needle, cast on 31 [33: 37: 39: 43: 45: 49: 51: 55] sts. Do *not* join; work back and forth in rows.

Work in K1, P1 rib as given for back for 6cm, ending with WS facing for the next row.

Dec row (WS): P1, (K1b, P1) 0 [1: 0: 1: 0: 1: 0: 1: 0] time, (S2KP, P1 K1b, P1) 5 [5: 6: 6: 7: 7: 8: 8: 9] times. 21 [23: 25: 27: 29: 31: 33: 35: 37] sts.

Change to 9mm (US 13) circular needle.

Beg with row 1, work in brioche rib patt as folls:

Cont straight until right front meas 38 [38: 38: 38: 39.5: 39.5: 41: 41: 41] cm, ending with RS facing for next row.

Place stitch marker at end of next RS row to denote start of armhole.

Cont straight until armhole meas 23 [24: 25.5: 25.5: 26.5 28: 28: 29: 30.5] cm from marker, ending WS facing for next row.

Shape shoulders

Cast off 10 [12: 14: 16: 18: 20: 22: 24: 26] sts sts at beg of next WS row. Place rem 11 sts on holder for neck.

SLEEVES

Using 7mm (US 10½) circular needle, cast on 33 [35: 33: 33: 35: 37: 37: 35: 37] sts. Do *not* join; work back and forth in rows.

Work in K1, P1 rib as given for back for 6cm, ending with RS facing for the next row.

Change to 9mm (US 13) circular needle.

Beg with row 1, work in brioche rib patt as folls:

Work in patt for 20 rows, ending with RS facing for next row.

Inc row (RS): K1, M2PK, patt to last st, M2KP, K1 (2 sts inc'd each end). 37 [39: 37: 37: 39: 41: 41: 39: 41] sts.

Rep inc row every foll - [-: -: 20th: 20th: 20th: 20th: 20th: 10th: 10th] row - [-: 1: 1: 1: 1: 1: 2: 2:] times more. 37 [39: 41: 41: 43: 45: 45: 47: 49] sts.

Cont straight until sleeve meas 44 [46: 46: 46: 46: 46: 48: 48: 48] cm, ending with RS facing for next row.

Cast off sts in patt.

MAKING UP

Block as described on information page.

Join shoulder seams using back stitch, or mattress stitch if preferred.

Hood

Next row (RS) Using 9mm (US 13) circular needle, patt 11 sts from right front holder, pick up and P1 in corner, patt first 10 sts from back neck holder, place marker, K1b (centre st), place marker, patt rem 10 sts from back neck holder, pick up and P1 in corner, patt 11 sts from left front holder. 45 sts (22 sts each side of centre st).

Next row (WS) Work brioche rib to marker, slip marker, P1, slip marker, work brioche rib to end.

Shape hood

Inc row (RS) Patt to marker, M2KP, slip marker, K1b, slip marker, M2PK, patt to end. 49 sts (2 sts increased each side of centre st).

Work 3 rows.

Rep last 4 rows twice more. 57 sts (28 sts each side of centre st).

Work straight until hood meas 34cm from pick-up row, ending with a WS facing for next row.

Dec row (WS) Patt to 3 sts before marker, S2KP, slip marker, P1, slip marker, Sk2P, patt to end. 53 sts (2 sts decreased each side of centre st).

Work 3 rows.

Rep last 4 rows twice more. 45 sts (22 sts each side of centre st).

Place first half of sts on a second needle and join open sts using 3-needle bind off.

3-needle bind-off

1. Hold right sides of pieces together on two needles. Insert third needle knitwise into first st of each needle, and wrap yarn knitwise.

2. Knit these two sts together, and slip them off the needles. *Knit the next two sts together in the same manner.

3. Slip first st on 3rd needle over 2nd st and off needle. Rep from * in step 2 across row until all sts are bound off.

Front and hood edging
Using one 9mm (US 13) circular needle, beg at lower right front edge, pick up and knit 52 [54: 55: 55: 57: 59: 60: 61: 62] sts along right front edge, then 34 sts along outer edge of hood to join; with second 9mm (US 13) circular needle, pick up and knit 34 sts along second half of hood, then 52 [54: 55: 55: 57: 59: 60: 61: 62] sts along left front edge. 172 [176: 178: 178: 182: 186: 188: 190: 192] sts. Cast off all sts knitwise.

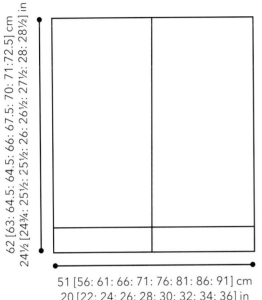

62 [63: 64.5: 64.5: 66: 67.5: 70: 71:72.5] cm
24½ [24¾: 25½: 25½: 26: 26½: 27½: 28: 28½] in

51 [56: 61: 66: 71: 76: 81: 86: 91] cm
20 [22: 24: 26: 28: 30: 32: 34: 36] in

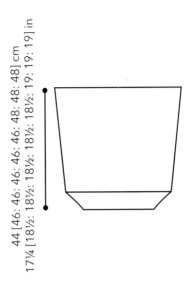

44 [46: 46: 46: 46: 48: 48: 48] cm
17¼ [18½: 18½: 18½: 18½: 19: 19: 19] in

cici
● ● ○ ○

SIZE
To fit bust

71-76	81-86	91-97	102-107	112-117	122-127	132-137	142-147	152-157	cm
28-30	32-34	36-38	40-42	44-46	48-50	52-54	56-58	60-62	in

Actual bust measurement of garment

90	102	110	121	130	142	150	162	172	cm
35½	40	43	48	51	56	59	64	67	in

YARN
Soft Boucle

7	7	8	8	9	9	10	10	11	x 50gm

(photographed in Natural 602)

NEEDLES
1 pair 6mm (no 4) (US 10) needles
1 x 6mm (no 4) (US 10) circular needle, 60cm/24in long

TENSION
14 sts and 24 rows to 10cm/4in measured over textured patt using 6mm (US 10) needles.

EXTRAS
Stitch holders

BACK

Using 6mm (US 10) needles, cast on 63 [71: 77: 85: 91: 99: 105: 113: 119] sts.
Row 1 (RS): Purl.
Row 2 (WS): K1, *yf, sl 1 purlwise, yb, K1, rep from * to end.
These 2 rows form textured patt.
Cont straight until back meas 40 [40. 41. 41. 42: 42: 43: 43: 44] cm, ending with RS facing for next row.

Shape armholes

Cast off 2 [2: 3: 2: 3: 4: 4: 6: 7] sts at beg of next 2 rows. 59 [67: 71: 81: 85: 91: 97: 101: 105] sts.
Work 2 rows.
Dec 1 st at each end of next and every foll 0 [0: 1: 1: 2: 2: 3: 4: 6] alt rows. 57 [65: 67: 77: 79: 85: 89: 91: 91] sts.
Cont straight until armhole meas 22 [23: 24: 24: 25.5: 25.5: 26.5: 28: 28] cm, ending with RS facing for next row.

Shape shoulders

Cast off 4 [4: 4: 5: 6: 6: 6: 6: 6] sts at beg of next 2 [10: 8: 10: 2: 6: 10: 10: 10] rows and 3 [0: 5: 0: 5: 5: 0: 0: 0] sts at beg of next 8 [0: 2: 0: 8: 4: 0: 0: 0] rows.
Place rem 25 [25: 25: 27: 27: 29: 29: 31: 31] sts on a st holder for back neck.

LEFT FRONT

Using 6mm (US 10) needles, cast on 33 [37: 40: 43: 47: 49: 53: 57: 61] sts.
Beg with row 1, work in textured patt as given for back as folls:
Work straight until left front meas 40 [40: 41: 41: 42: 42: 43: 43: 44] cm, ending with RS facing for next row.

Shape armhole

Next row (RS): Cast off 2 [2: 3: 2: 3: 4: 4: 6: 7] sts, work to end. 31 [35: 37: 41: 44: 45: 49: 51: 54] sts.
Work 3 rows.
Dec 1 st at beg of next and every foll 0 [0: 1: 1: 2: 2: 3: 4: 6] alt rows. 30 [34: 35: 39: 41: 42: 45: 46: 47] sts.
Cont straight until armhole meas 22 [23: 24: 24: 25.5: 25.5: 26.5: 28: 28] cm, ending with RS facing for next row.

Shape shoulders

Next row (RS): Cast off 4 [4: 4: 5: 6: 6: 6: 6: 6] sts, work to end. 26 [30: 31: 34: 35: 36: 39: 40: 41] sts.
Cont to cast off 0 [4: 4: 5: 6: 6: 6: 6: 6] sts at beg of foll 0 [4: 3: 4: 0: 2: 4: 4: 4] alt rows, then 3 [0: 5: 0: 5: 5: 0: 0: 0] sts at beg of foll 4 [0: 1: 0: 4: 2: 0: 0: 0] alt rows.
Place rem 14 [14: 14: 14: 15: 14: 15: 16: 17] sts on a holder for neck.

RIGHT FRONT

Using 6mm (US 10) needles, cast on 33 [37: 40: 43: 47: 49: 53: 57: 61] sts.
Beg with row 1, work in textured patt as given for back as folls:
Work straight until right front meas 40 [40: 41: 41: 42: 42: 43: 43: 44] cm, ending with WS facing for next row.

Shape armhole

Next row (WS): Cast off 2 [2: 3: 2: 3: 4: 4: 6: 7] sts, work to end. 31 [35: 37: 41: 44: 45: 49: 51: 54] sts.
Work 2 rows.
Dec 1 st at end of next and every foll 0 [0: 1: 1: 2: 2: 3: 4: 6] alt rows. 30 [34: 35: 39: 41: 42: 45: 46: 47] sts.
Cont straight until armhole meas 22 [23: 24: 24: 25.5: 25.5: 26.5: 28: 28] cm, ending with WS facing for next row.

Shape shoulders

Next row (WS): Cast off 4 [4: 4: 5: 6: 6: 6: 6: 6] sts, work to end. 26 [30: 31: 34: 35: 36: 39: 40: 41] sts.
Cont to cast off 4 [4: 4: 5: 6: 6: 6: 6: 6] sts at beg of foll 0 [4: 3: 4: 0: 2: 4: 4: 4] alt rows, then 3 [0: 5: 0: 5: 5: 0: 0: 0] sts at beg of foll 4 [0: 1: 0: 4: 2: 0: 0: 0] alt rows.
Place rem 14 [14: 14: 14: 15: 14: 15: 16: 17] sts on a holder for neck.

MAKING UP

Block as described on information page.

Join shoulder seams using back stitch, or mattress stitch if preferred.

Hood

With RS facing and using 6mm (US 10) circular needle, P14 [14: 14: 14: 15: 14: 15: 16: 17] sts from right front holder, work sts from back neck holder as foll: P12 [12: 12: 13: 13: 14: 14: 15: 15], place marker, P1 (centre st), place marker, P12 [12: 12: 13: 13: 14: 14: 15: 15]; then P14 [14: 14: 14: 15: 14: 15: 16: 17] sts from left front holder. 53 [53: 53: 55: 57: 57: 59: 63: 65] sts. Do *not* join; work back and forth in rows.

Next row (WS): Work row 2 of textured patt as given for back to marker, slip marker, K1, slip marker, work row 2 of textured patt as set for back to end.

Shape hood

Inc row (RS): P to marker, M1-P, slip marker, P1, slip marker, M1-P, P to end (2 sts increased in centre).

Next row (WS): Work row 2 of textured patt as given, working inc'd sts into patt.

Rep last 2 rows until there are 71 [71: 71: 71: 73: 73: 73: 75: 75] sts in total. (35 [35: 35: 35: 36: 36: 36: 37: 37] sts each side of centre st).

Cont straight until hood measures 34cm from pick-up row, ending with RS facing for next row.

Dec row (RS): P to 2 sts before marker, P2tog, slip marker, P1, slip marker, P2tog, P to end. (2 sts decreased in centre).

Next row (WS): Work row 2 of textured patt as set.

Rep last 2 rows 3 times more, ending with WS facing for next row. 63 [63: 63: 63: 65: 65: 65: 67: 67] sts.

Last row (WS): P to marker, remove marker, P2tog, remove marker, P to end. 62 [62: 62: 62: 64: 64: 64: 66: 66] sts.

Place first half of sts on a second needle and join open sts using 3-needle bind-off.

3-needle bind-off

1. Hold right sides of pieces together on two needles. Insert third needle knitwise into first st of each needle, and wrap yarn knitwise.

2. Knit these two sts together, and slip them off the needles. *Knit the next two sts together in the same manner.

3. Slip first st on 3rd needle over 2nd st and off needle. Rep from * in step 2 across row until all sts are bound off.

Hood lining

With WS of hood facing and using 6mm (US 10) circular needle, working along inside edge of first row of main hood and beg at left front neck edge, pick up and knit 14 [14: 14: 14: 15: 14: 15: 16: 17] sts along left front neck, 25 [25: 25: 27: 27: 29: 29: 31: 31] sts along back neck, 14 [14: 14: 14: 15: 14: 15: 16: 17] sts along right front neck. 53 [53: 53: 55: 57: 57: 59: 63: 65] sts. Do *not* join; work back and forth in rows.

Next row (WS of hood lining): Work row 2 of textured patt as given for back over first 26 [26: 26: 27: 28: 28: 29: 31: 32] sts, place marker, K1 (centre st), place marker, work row 2 of textured patt as given for back over last 26 [26: 26: 27: 28: 28: 29: 31: 32] sts.

Complete same as main hood.

Join outer edges of hood lining to main hood.

Join side seams.

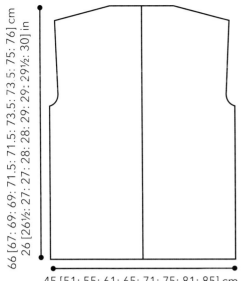

66 [67: 69: 69: 71.5: 71.5: 73.5: 73.5: 75: 76] cm
26 [26½: 27: 27: 28: 28: 29: 29: 29½: 30] in

45 [51: 55: 61: 65: 71: 75: 81: 85] cm
17¾: [20: 21¾: 24: 25½: 28: 29½: 32: 33½] in

margo
●●○○

SIZE
To fit bust

71-76	81-86	91-97	102-107	112-117	122-127	132-137	142-147	152-157	cm
28-30	32-34	36-38	40-42	44-46	48-50	52-54	56-58	60-62	in

Actual bust measurement of garment

78	87	98	109	118	129	138	149	158	cm
30¾	34¼	38½	43	46½	50¾	54¼	58¾	62¼	in

YARN
Alpaca Soft DK

12	13	13	14	14	15	15	16	16	x 50gm

(photographed in Classic Brown 204)

NEEDLES
1 pair 3¼mm (no 10) (US 3) needles
1 pair 4mm (no 8) (US 6) needles
1 x 4mm (no 8) (US 6) circular needle, 80cm/32in long

TENSION
22 stitches and 30 rows to 10cm/4in measured over st st using 4mm (US 6) needles.

EXTRAS
Stitch holders
Stitch markers

BACK

Using 3¼mm (US 3) needles, cast on 106 [114: 124: 134: 146: 158: 172: 184: 194] sts.

Row 1 (RS): *K1, P1, rep from * to end.

Row 2 (WS): *P1, K1, rep from * to end.

These 2 rows form moss st patt.

Rep last 2 rows twice more.

Change to 4mm (US 6) needles.

Beg with a K row, cont in st st throughout as folls:

Work 2 rows, ending with RS facing for next row.

Next row (RS): K2, Sl 1, K1, psso, K to last 4 sts, K2tog, K2. 104 [112: 122: 132: 144: 156: 170: 182: 192] sts.

Working dec as set above, cont in st st, dec 1 st at each end of every foll 14th [16th: 18th: 20th: 18th: 18th: 16th: 14th: 14th] row to 86 [96: 108: 120: 130: 142: 152: 164: 174] sts.

Cont straight until back meas 51 [51: 52: 52: 53: 53: 54: 54: 55] cm, ending with RS facing for next row.

Place a stitch marker at each end of next RS row to denote start of armholes.

Shape armholes

Next row (RS): K2, Sl 1, K1, psso, K to last 4 sts, K2tog, K2. 84 [94: 106: 118: 128: 140: 150: 162: 172] sts.

Work 3 rows.

Rep last 4 rows to 78 [88: 100: 112: 122: 134: 144: 156: 166] sts.

Cont straight until armhole meas 22 [22.5: 24: 25.5: 27: 29: 31: 32: 32.5] cm from markers, ending with RS facing for next row.

Shape shoulders and back neck

Next row (RS): K26 [31: 36: 42: 46: 52: 56: 62: 66], turn.

Next row (WS): P2, P2tog, P to end. 25 [30: 35: 41: 45: 51: 55: 61: 65] sts.

Next row: Cast off 15 [20: 25: 31: 35: 41: 45: 51: 55] sts, K to end. 10 sts.

Cast off.

With RS facing, slip centre 26 [26: 28: 28: 30: 30: 32: 32: 34] sts onto a second stitch holder, rejoin yarn to rem sts and K to end.

Work as for other side of neck, reversing shapings.

LEFT FRONT

Using 3¼mm (US 3) needles, cast on 124 [132: 142: 154: 164: 176: 190: 202: 212] sts.

Work in moss st as given for back for 4 rows, ending with RS facing for next row.

Change to 4mm (US 6) needles.

Beg with a K row, cont in st st throughout as folls:

Work 2 rows, ending with RS facing for next row.

Next row (RS): K2, Sl 1, K1, psso, K to end. 123 [131: 141: 153: 163: 175: 189: 201: 211] sts.

Working dec as set above, cont in st st, dec 1 st at side edge of every foll 14th [16th: 18th: 20th: 18th: 18th: 16th: 14th: 14th] row to 114 [124: 134: 146: 156: 168: 180: 192: 203] sts.

Cont straight until left front meas 51 [51: 52: 52: 53: 53: 54: 54: 55] cm, ending with RS facing for next row.

Place a stitch marker at beg of next RS row to denote start of armhole.

Shape armhole

Next row (RS): K2, Sl 1, K1, psso, K to end. 113 [123: 133: 145: 155: 167: 179: 191: 202] sts.

Work 3 rows.

Rep last 4 rows to 106 [116: 126: 138: 148: 160: 176: 188: 199] sts.

Cont straight until armhole meas 22 [22.5: 24: 25.5: 27: 29: 31: 32: 32.5] cm from marker, ending with WS facing for next row. Break off yarn.

Shape shoulder and front neck

Next row (WS): Slip next 81 [86: 91: 97: 103: 109: 121: 127: 134] sts onto a stitch holder, rejoin yarn and P to end. 25 [30: 35: 41: 45: 51: 55: 61: 65] sts.

Next row (RS): Knit.

Next row: Cast off 15 [20: 25: 31: 35: 41: 45: 51: 55] sts, P to end. 10 sts.

Cast off.

RIGHT FRONT

Using 3¼mm (US 3) needles, cast on 124 [132 142: 154 164: 176: 190: 202: 212] sts.
Work in moss st as given for back for 4 rows, ending with RS facing for next row.
Change to 4mm (US 6) needles.
Beg with a K row, cont in st st throughout as folls:
Work 2 rows, ending with RS facing for next row.
Next row (RS): K to last 4 sts, K2tog, K2. 123 [131: 141: 153: 163: 175: 189: 201: 211] sts.
Working dec as set above, cont in st st, dec 1 st at side edge of every foll 14th [16th: 18th: 20th: 18th: 18th: 16th: 14th: 14th] row to 114 [124: 134: 146: 156: 168: 180: 192: 203] sts.
Cont straight until right front meas 51 [51: 52: 52: 53: 53: 54: 54: 55] cm, ending with RS facing for next row.
Place a stitch marker at end of next RS row to denote start of armhole.

Shape armhole
Next row (RS): K to last 4 sts, K2tog, K2. 113 [123: 133: 145: 155: 167: 179: 191: 202] sts.
Work 3 rows.
Rep last 4 rows to 106 [116: 126: 138: 148: 160: 176: 188: 199] sts.
Cont straight until armhole meas 22 [22.5: 24: 25.5: 27: 29: 31: 32: 32.5] cm from marker, ending with RS facing for next row. Break off yarn.

Shape shoulder and front neck
Next row (RS): Slip next 81 [86: 91: 97: 103: 109: 121: 127: 134] sts onto a stitch holder, rejoin yarn and K to end. 25 [30: 35: 41: 45: 51: 55: 61: 65] sts.
Next row (WS): Purl.
Next row: Cast off 15 [20: 25: 31: 35: 41: 45: 51: 55] sts, K to end. 10 sts.
Cast off.

MAKING UP

Press as described on the information page.
Join both shoulder seams using mattress stitch.

Neckband
With RS facing and using 4mm (US 6) circular needle, K81 [86: 91: 97: 103: 109: 121: 127: 134] sts from right front stitch holder, pick up and knit 3 sts down right back neck, K26 [26: 28: 28: 30: 30: 32: 32: 34] sts from back neck stitch holder, pick up and knit 3 sts up left back neck, K81 [86: 91: 97: 103: 109: 121: 127: 134] sts from left front stitch holder. 194 [204: 216: 228: 242: 254: 280: 292: 308] sts.
Do *not* join; work back and forth in rows.
Row 1 (WS): Purl.
Row 2 (RS): Knit.
These 2 rows form rev st st.
Cont in rev st st for 8cm, ending with RS facing for next row.
Cast off loosely knitwise.
Join side seams.

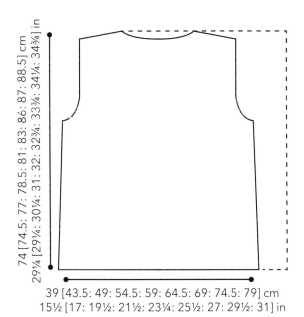

74 [74.5: 77: 78.5: 81: 83: 86: 87: 88.5] cm
29¼ [29¼: 30¼: 31: 32: 32¾: 33¾: 34¼: 34¾] in

39 [43.5: 49: 54.5: 59: 64.5: 69: 74.5: 79] cm
15½ [17: 19½: 21½: 23¼: 25½: 27: 29½: 31] in

48 [52: 56.5: 61: 66.5: 72: 78: 83.5: 88] cm
19 [20½: 22¼: 24: 26¼: 28¼: 30¾: 32¾: 34¾] in

noelle

● ● ○ ○

SIZE
To fit bust

71-76	81-86	91-97	102-107	112-117	122-127	132-137	142-147	152-157	cm
28-30	32-34	36-38	40-42	44-46	48-50	52-54	56-58	60-62	in

Actual bust measurement of garment

90	101	109	120	131	141	149	160	170	cm
36	40	43	47	51½	55½	59	63	67	in

YARN
Felted Tweed Aran

14	14	15	15	16	16	17	17	18	x 50gm

(photographed in Pine 782)

NEEDLES
1 pair 4½mm (US 7) needles
1 x 4½mm (US 7) circular needle, 80cm/32in long

TENSION
19 sts and 25 rows to 10cm/4in measured over st st using 4½mm (US 7) needles.

EXTRAS
Stitch holders
Stitch markers

BACK

Using 4½mm (US 7) needles, cast on 86 [96: 104: 114: 124: 134: 142: 152: 162] sts.
Beg with a K row, cont in st st throughout as folls:
Cont straight until back meas 46 [47: 47: 47: 47: 48: 48: 48: 48] cm, ending with RS facing for next row.
Place stitch marker each end of next RS row to denote the start of armholes.
Cont straight until armhole meas 19 [19.5: 20.5: 22: 22.5: 22.5: 23.5: 24: 25.5] cm from markers, ending with RS facing for next row.

Shape shoulders
Cast off 7 [8: 9: 10: 11: 12: 13: 14: 15] sts at beg of next 4 [4: 4: 4: 2: 2: 4: 2: 2] rows and 8 [9: 10: 11: 12: 13: 14: 15: 16] sts at beg of next 4 [4: 4: 4: 6: 6: 4: 6: 6] rows. Place rem 26 [28: 28: 30: 30: 32: 34: 34: 36] sts on holder for back neck.

LEFT FRONT

Using 4½mm (US 7) needles, cast on 65 [73: 79: 86: 94: 101: 107: 115: 122] sts.
Row 1 (RS): K43 [48: 52: 57: 62: 67: 71: 76: 81], place marker, P1 (turning ridge), K21 [24: 26: 28: 31: 33: 35: 38: 40] for facing.
Row 2 (WS): P21 [24: 26: 28: 31: 33: 35: 38: 40] for facing, K1 (turning ridge), P43 [48: 52: 57: 62: 67: 71: 76: 81].
These 2 rows form patt.
Work in patt throughout as folls:
Cont straight in patt until left front meas 46 [47: 47: 47: 47: 48: 48: 48: 48] cm, ending with RS facing for next row.
Place marker at beg of next RS row to denote start of armhole.
Cont straight until armhole measures 19 [19.5: 20.5: 22: 22.5: 22.5: 23.5: 24: 25.5] cm from markers, ending with WS facing for next row.
Next row (WS): Cast off 22 [25: 27: 29: 32: 34: 36: 39: 41] sts (facing sts plus turning st), purl to end. 43 [48: 52: 57: 62: 67: 71: 76: 81] sts.

Shape shoulder
Cast off 7 [8: 9: 10: 11: 12: 13: 14: 15] sts, 2 [2: 2: 2: 1: 1: 2: 1: 1] times and 8 [9: 10: 11: 12: 13: 14: 15: 16] sts 2 [2: 2: 2: 3: 3: 2: 3: 3] times.
Place rem 13 [14: 14: 15: 15: 16: 17: 17: 18] sts on holder for neck.

RIGHT FRONT

Using 4½mm (US 7) needles, cast on 65 [73: 79: 86: 94: 101: 107: 115: 122] sts.
Row 1 (RS): K21 [24: 26: 28: 31: 33: 35: 38: 40] for facing, place marker, P1 (turning ridge), K43 [48: 52: 57: 62: 67: 71: 76: 81].
Row 2 (WS): P43 [48: 52: 57: 62: 67: 71: 76: 81], K1 (turning ridge), P21 [24: 26: 28: 31: 33: 35: 38: 40] for facing.
These 2 rows form patt.
Work in patt throughout as folls:
Cont straight in patt until left front meas 46 [47: 47: 47: 47: 48: 48: 48: 48] cm, ending with RS facing for next row.
Place marker at end of next (RS) row to denote the start of armhole.
Cont straight until armhole 19 [19.5: 20.5: 22: 22.5: 22.5: 23.5: 24: 25.5] cm from markers, ending with RS facing for next row.
Next row (RS): Cast off 22 [25: 27: 29: 32: 34: 36: 39: 41] sts (facing sts plus turning st), purl to end. 43 [48: 52: 57: 62: 67: 71: 76: 81] sts.

Shape shoulder
Cast off 7 [8: 9: 10: 11: 12: 13: 14: 15] sts 2 [2: 2: 2: 1: 1: 2: 1: 1] times and 8 [9: 10: 11: 12: 13: 14: 15: 16] sts 2 [2: 2: 2: 3: 3: 2: 3: 3] times.
Place rem 13 [14: 14: 15: 15: 16: 17: 17: 18] sts on holder for neck.

SLEEVES

Using 4½mm (US 7) needles, cast on 42 [42: 42: 44: 44: 46: 46: 48: 48] sts.
Beg with a K row, work in st st for 8 rows.
Turning ridge row (RS): Purl.
Beg with a P row (WS), work in st st for 8 rows more, end with WS facing for next row.
Joining row (WS): Fold cast-on edge up to sts on needle, insert RH needle into first cast-on st and place on LH needle, P these 2 sts tog. Cont in this way until all cast-on sts are joined to the sts on LH needle.
Cont in st st, inc 1 st each end of next and every foll 6th row to 72 [74: 78: 66: 66: 68: 62: 64: 52] sts, then every foll 4th row to - [-: -: 84: 86: 86: 90: 92: 98] sts.
Cont straight until sleeve meas 45cm, ending with RS facing for next row.
Cast off all sts loosely.

MAKING UP

Block as described on information page.
Join shoulder seams using back stitch, or mattress stitch if preferred.
Fold front facings to WS at turning ridge and sew in place.

Collar

With RS facing and using 4½mm (US 7) circular needle, beg at right front neck edge, knit 13 [14: 14: 15: 15: 16: 17: 17, 18] sts from right front holder, 26 [28: 28: 30: 30: 32: 34: 34: 36] sts from back neck holder and 13 [14: 14: 15: 15: 16: 17: 17, 18] sts from left front holder. 52 [56: 56: 60: 60: 64: 68: 68: 72] sts. Do *not* join; work back and forth in rows.
Beg with a P row, work in st st for 12 rows.
Turning ridge row (WS): Knit.
Beg with a K row, work in st st for 12 rows.
Cast off.
Fold collar in half at turning ridge to WS and sew cast-off edge around neck edge.

Pockets (make 2)

Using 4½mm (US 7) needles, cast on 29 sts.
Beg with a K row, work in st st for 15cm, ending with RS facing for next row.
Cast off sts loosely.
Sew pocket to each front at 4cm from lower edge and 5cm in from front edge.
Sew top of sleeve to front and back between armhole markers. Join side and sleeve seams.

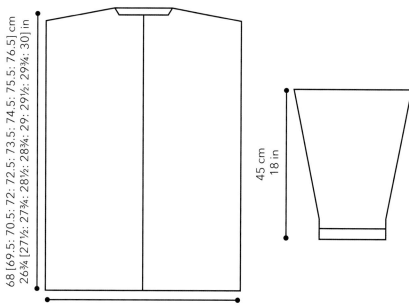

68 [69.5: 70.5: 72: 72.5: 73.5: 74.5: 75.5: 76.5] cm
26¾ [27½: 27¾: 28½: 28¾: 29: 29½: 29¾: 30] in

45 cm
18 in

45 [50.5: 54.5: 60: 65.5: 70.5: 74.5: 80: 85] cm
17¾ [20: 21½: 23½: 25¾: 27¾: 29½: 31½: 33½] in

SIZING

We have recently increased our size range to help you achieve the best fit for your knitwear. Our womenswear sizes now range from 28"/71cm through to 62"/157cm across the chest.

Dimensions in the charts below are body measurements, not garment dimensions. Therefore, please refer to the measuring guide to help you to determine which is the best size for you to knit.

STANDARD SIZING GUIDE FOR WOMEN

To fit bust

28-30	32-34	36-38	40-42	44-46	48-50	52-54	56-58	60-62	inches
71-76	81-86	91-97	102-107	112-117	122-127	132-137	142-147	152-157	cm

To fit waist

20-22	24-26	28-30	32-34	36-38	40-42	44-46	48-50	52-54	inches
51-56	61-66	71-76	81-86	91-97	102-107	112-117	122-127	132-137	cm

To fit hips

30-31	34-36	38-40	42-44	46-48	50-52	54-56	58-60	62-64	inches
76-81	86-91	97-102	107-112	117-122	127-132	137-142	147-152	157-162	cm

SIZING & SIZE DIAGRAM NOTE

The instructions are given for the smallest size. Where they vary, work the figures in brackets for the larger sizes. One set of figures refers to all sizes.

Included with most patterns is a size diagram; see image below of the finished garment and its dimensions. The measurement shown at the bottom of each size diagram shows the garment width. The size diagram will also indicate how the garment is constructed. For example, if the garment has a drop shoulder, this will be reflected in the drawing.

To help you choose the size of garment to knit, please refer to the sizing guide. Generally, in the majority of designs, the welt width (at the cast-on edge of the garment) is the same width as the chest.

If you don't want to measure yourself, note the size of a similar shaped garment that you own and compare it with the size diagram given at the end of the pattern.

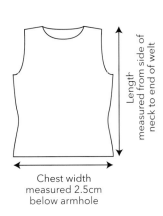

Chest width
measured 2.5cm
below armhole

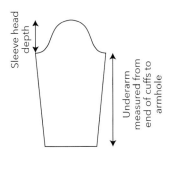

MEASURING GUIDE

For maximum comfort and to ensure the correct fit when choosing a size to knit, please follow the tips below when checking your size. Measure yourself close to your body, over your underwear, and don't pull the tape measure too tight!

Bust/chest | measure around the fullest part of the bust/chest and across the shoulder blades.

Waist | measure around the natural waistline, just above the hip bones.

Hips | measure around the fullest part of the bottom.

Finally, once you have decided which size is best for you, please ensure that you achieve the tension required for the design you wish to knit.

Remember, if your tension is too loose, your garment will be bigger than the pattern size and you may use more yarn. If your tension is too tight, your garment could be smaller than the pattern size and you will have yarn left over.

Furthermore, if your tension is incorrect, the handle of your fabric will be too stiff or floppy and will not fit properly. It really does make sense to check your tension before starting every project.

PHOTOGRAPHY MODEL SIZING

The model used in this collection wears a UK dress size 10. Garments were knitted in bust size 32 - 34". Height: 175cm / 5ft 9in

TENSION

This is the size of your knitting. Most of the knitting patterns will have a tension quoted. This is how many stitches 10cm/4in in width and how many rows 10cm/4in in length to make a square. If your knitting doesn't match this, then your finished garment will not measure the correct size. To obtain the correct measurements for your garment, you must achieve the tension.

The tension quoted on a ball band is the manufacturer's average. For the manufacturer and designers to produce designs, they have to use a tension for you to be able to obtain the measurements quoted. It's fine not to be the average, but you need to know if you meet the average or not. Then you can make the necessary adjustments to obtain the correct measurements.

CHOOSING YARN

All the colours and textures, where do you start? Look for the thickness - how chunky do you want your finished garment? Sometimes it's colour that draws you to a yarn, or perhaps you have a pattern that requires a specific yarn. Check the washing/care instructions before you buy.

Yarn varies in thickness; there are various descriptions, such as DK and 4ply. These are examples of standard weights. There are a lot of yarns available that are not standard, so it helps to read the ball band to see what the recommended needle size is.

This will give you an idea of the approximate thickness. It is best to use the yarn recommended in the pattern.
Keep one ball band from each project so that you have a record of what you have used, and most importantly, how to care for your garment after it has been completed. Always remember to give the ball band with the garment if it is a gift.

The ball band normally provides you with the average tension and recommended needle sizes for the yarn, this may vary from what has been used in the pattern, always go with the pattern as the designer may change needles to obtain a certain look. The ball band also tells you the name of the yarn and what it is made of, the weight and approximate length of the ball of yarn, along with the shade and dye lot numbers. This is important as dye lots can vary, so you need to buy your yarn with matching dye lots.

PRESSING AND AFTERCARE

Having spent so long knitting your project, it can be a great shame not to look after it properly. Some yarns are suitable for pressing once you have finished to improve the look of the fabric. To find out this information, you will need to look on the yarn ball band, where there will be washing and care symbols.

Once you have checked to see if your yarn is suitable to be pressed and the knitting is a smooth texture (stocking stitch, for example), pin out and place a damp cloth onto the knitted pieces. Hold the steam iron (at the correct temperature) approximately 10cm/4in away from the fabric and steam. Keep the knitted pieces pinned in place until cool.

As a test, it is a good idea to wash your tension square in the way you would expect to wash your garment.

EXPERIENCE RATING
(for guidance only)

● **BEGINNER TECHNIQUES**

For the beginner knitter, basic garment shaping and straight forward stitch technique.

● ● **SIMPLE TECHNIQUES**

Simple straight forward knitting, introducing various shaping techniques and garments.

● ● ● **EXPERIENCED TECHNIQUES**

For the more experienced knitter, using more advanced shaping techniques at the same time as colourwork or different stitch techniques.

● ● ● ● **ADVANCED TECHNIQUES**

Advanced techniques used, including advanced stitches and garment shaping.

ABBREVIATIONS

alt	alternate
beg	begin(ning)
cm	centimetres
cont	continue
dec	decrease(s)(ing)
foll(s)	follow(s)(ing)
g	grams
g st	garter stitch (knit all rows)
in	inch(es)
inc	increase(s)(ing)
K	knit
Kfb	knit in front and back of stitch (makes 1 stitch)
M1	make 1 stitch
meas	measures
mm	millimetres
P	purl
patt	pattern
psso	pass slipped stitch over
rem	remain(ing)
rep	repeat
RS	right side of work
Sl 1	slip 1 stitch
st st	stocking stitch (knit on RS rows, purl on WS rows)
st(s)	stitch(es)
tbl	through back of loop
tog	together
WS	wrong side of work

quail studio